PRAISE FOR
say, said

"In *say, said,* Fred Dale's poetry offers a nuanced exploration of memory, identity, and existential uncertainty, using both personal and cosmic registers. With lyrical complexity, Dale's work examines the interplay of gender, familial bonds, and the darker contours of the human psyche. The poems are infused with a compelling blend of the corporeal and the metaphysical, where themes of loss, transformation, and the forces that shape existence are brought to the fore, where speakers are "scraping / the wells of our reserves to survive." Through a fragmented narrative structure, Dale interrogates the tension between self-conception and external forces, while interrogating the hidden histories that form our collective consciousness, often in memorably imagistic ways ("a fragrance encircled by star flowers"). Like the river he writes of in "tonight's the night" ("so much of [it] we never know while we're in it"), Dale's work is immersive, startling, and profound. The result is a collection that challenges the boundaries of form and meaning, urging readers to reflect on the spaces between memory and myth, destruction and creation."

—Liz Robbins,
author of *Freaked*

"There's a man in full—lives first, writes second—in this book, these poems. His name is Fred Dale, the same as on the cover. Poetry, for him, is language in its finer tunings. His company is worth your keeping."

—William Slaughter,
author of *The Politics of My Heart* and *Untold Stories*

"From the gates, Fred Dale declares that the brain will "not tell you about the pain that's coming," and here in this ecological moment reminiscent of biblical times, where the dead are "picked from us like burrs," and memories of the past form brackish water with the present, *say, said,* holds tender testimony to the remarkable treasures and wounds of the everyday. So fine is Dale's attunement and movement between the natural and human worlds: the insides of trees, "a gentleman in an unwinding tux," a marsh hawk. I would have highlighted this whole book if only that wouldn't make it harder for me to reread or offer as a balm for others to read. This lyric wrests me from despair and reorients me toward the hard-won remarkability of wonder."

—Diana Khoi Nguyen,
author of *Ghost Of* and *Root Fractures*

"Fred Dale's *say, said* is a terrific, nervy collection that parses distance between present and past as an opportunity for personal and formal revelation. These poems channel pathos that will resonate for any grown child who has paused to stare at the contents of their parent's grocery cart. Yet Dale's poems think expansively as well—poking fingers into the honeycomb of wonder, seeking 'a sheep's worth of sunlight,' interrogating the soul as a dinosaur bone afloat in the sea of time—and restlessly flash their sly wit through intriguing titles and unexpected imagery. This is a marvel of a book."

—Sandra Beasley,
author of *Made to Explode*

say, said

fred dale

Independently published by *Driftwood Press*
in the United States of America.

Managing Poetry Editor & Interviewer: Sara Moore Wagner
Cover Image: Nate Hill
Cover Design: Sally Franckowiak
Interior Design: James McNulty
Fonts: Knockout, Merriweather,
& Alternate Gothic Extra Condensed

Copyright © 2026 by Fred Dale
All Rights Reserved.

No part of this publication
may be reproduced, stored in a retrieval
program, or transmitted, in any form or by
any means (electronic, mechanical,
photographic, recording, etc.), without
the publisher's written permission.

First published January 27, 2026
ISBN-13: 978-1-949065-40-4
Please visit our website at www.driftwoodpress.com
or email us at editor@driftwoodpress.net.

CONTENTS

tonight's the night	1
what the florentine hid from us	2
agnes in the flood	3
home is a hyoid	4
she who carries the water, carries the fish	5
other inherited things	7
we are told bay leaves	8
rock by rock	9
abattoir	10
children	11
steering wheels on publix carts	12
st. edna and the thieves	13
sweatshirt of bees	14
a hive for water	16
a heralding	17
fishing poem	18
teach violinists to stage dive	20
take five	21
falling is the last resort of squirrels	22
magnolias	23
the boy who would be pope	24
downs lounge	25
geometric matter(s)	26
a barstool at st. nick's	27
saliva's point of jumping off	28
motorboat mels	29
tin ceiling sky	30
gifts of unexpected conveyances	31
the luminaria sleep	32
everything from one	33
bartram heard it	34
drawn bird	35

starling	36
a place to sit a spell	37
three minutes	39
marsh hawk	40
roadkill bingo	42
if you need a revolution, dee dee ramone'll count you down	43
shadow puppets	44
triangle tavern, astoria	45
what we picked on our way	46
meteors over hurricane ridge	48
a valley away/ hailey, idaho	49
a coin awaits a sailor	50
vagary	51
these trails never wanted us	52
trails in our legs	53
mid-november flower	54
ben nevis	55
north unit, t. r. n. p.	56
acorn tattoo	57
marriage house	58
daycare in the garden of good children	59
waiting to speak	60
Interview: The Reliquaries That Hold a Past I Need Within Reach	63

For Valerie, the love in here I learned from you.

And I rose
In rainy autumn
And walked abroad in a shower of all my days.

— Dylan Thomas, "Poem in October"

tonight's the night

might be a photograph of me in drag as a teen. we shouldered up on halloween—a ninja, a proctologist, a werewolf. ninja flipped a coin to see who'd drop first, test the turbulence, report back. my mother said, rolling on the mascara, lovely lashes, son, our secret—she without daughters. she saying, i have only men to offer. let's rebuild the second child, the one who shut down business. a chance to talk out the miscarriage. a big bang blooming in my eyes. the answer to the question of why paint a bowl of red apples red is driving 10mph on i-10 on red star acid. i said, take the rest. you're gonna like the strychnine's bite. might have driven to a mossy cemetery, danced ourselves ghost oak soft. might have stopped on the tracks with a train coming. turned off the ignition. dropped the keys to the floorboard and screamed, go go go to the horn blast of first light. so much of the river we never know while we're in it, our dead picked from us like burrs. long before man was flung from the potter's wheel, at the thought of her powered-down eye, the creator held back their only daughter, said, tell them darkness was our first home.

what the florentine hid from us

stick in your pocket the discovery of michelangelo's thumbprint found on a wax statue not meant to survive, a model for the tomb of pope julius ii. think also of his ceiling work, where god's finger offers to adam the biometric delivery system for the whole she-bang, the schematics of life transferred with a touch. we are told faith is enough, but thomas didn't lose favor when he stuck his index finger inside the wily savior and pulled out combs of honey. god discovered, to sell the dogma, every hero needs a grieving mother. imagine a child without disciples, or a boy who did not require a resurrection. in the fresco-secco, the almighty's straining for contact, but adam's hand's a kind of hanging whatever. adam says, i didn't ask to be made. and god, a whole mess of angels on his shoulders, says, don't worry. you ain't my son. you're only the model, a mark-up destined for samael's furnace. be thankful for this miracle. you are here to witness the moment electricity learns to jump. there's a garden and a woman to take the blame.

agnes in the flood

as the levees released their boundless children and called her home, she popped back through the uncapped grave like a killer whale, learned everlastingness was love giving up on the rumor of the sea, and set sail across a land the chitimacha were wise not to settle on. adrift, she prayed to saint adjutor for deliverance. he said, you ask too much. this city's under the providence of water—a lake, a gulf and a river at war. goodness knows the mississippi wants to side-step the banquettes of new orleans, ramble straight to the atchafalaya basin, scrub clean the catfish and cottonmouths. jean lafitte foresaw the approaching breach, snuffed out the smithy, shipped off his mystique to barataria, said, when the barroom door closes behind you and the morning's out, stretching its back, you'll understand why the river wants gone. but not all's lost. the patron of the throat, st. blaise, is there to dislodge the bones stuck in the city's neck. he said, when the pepper-hot match presses against the soft albumen of your arm, the brain goes silent, thinks, i'll not tell you about the pain that's coming— st. christopher said, let this river mull its ambition. let these sidewalks turn back to riverboats. the silver anniversary dish of gumdrops is safe and the grandkids recall your buttered toast like heaven. this flood has little to do with saints, agnes. the faithful ripped us apart for relics.

home is hyoid

I.

be weird if/ like trees/ things took refuge in us as we fell apart/ a red-bellied woodpecker stalking the open-door circle of her nest/ entrance smooth as cannon muzzle/ the flute-full ruckus of tiny beaks/ the empty bell that held them the first season/ she thinks/ we are citizens of abandoned mothers/ when you mimic us/ you get the tune right/ but you can't fathom the implications of the song you sing/ decant this tree's lived-in memory/ build me a day of bugs/ i'm as unknowable as love/ as we emptied the cup of maw-maw's house/ she said/ son/ grab a keepsake from my sinking life/ the sacred heart of jesus/ a windbreak of daylilies/ survey his miles of morning/

II.

the hospice nurse said/ we're shotgun houses god sees straight through/ your paw-paw needs us to change him/ the wife who knows best this hidden territory/ his daughters/ they're out of range/ he's reaching for his mother when he raises his arm like he's volunteering for pearl diving/ she said/ each death's the first of its kind/ his cord to the side/ he might be a mountain/ or a tooth in the cotton/ his skinlight distinguishing the way/ i took the mirror/ the one hanging in the wedding photo of my mother/ where the gown whirls round her/ a spiral fracture of fabrics/ a future of children swirled to knots on a spoon/ a port where silky anteaters enter us without knocking

she who carries the water, carries the fish

through the hands and the gut, the sunken child tells

you what kind of fish she'll be.

only this one snaps the line as she comes into view,

a miscarried shape that speaks your name.

when the cork remains on the surface, moving away,

you realize it's a finger pointing

to the fish below, and you tell him this is the fish you

need, a sister. so, the father

hauls the anchor, releases the boat. carried by water,

their minds drift to the mother,

the dead child induced from her, the stolen little one

the doctors brought to the surface,

the gutting of the mother who tried again, regardless,

and won another son,

learning—she who carries the water, carries the fish.

and the father, years later on a trail,

will tell you he wept buckets—that pain, like water,

finds its way into us, that people are

a kind of water. but before assembling this enormity

for a walk, the boy's reached the bobber,

too bloody dumb to discern the cork will slide free,

that the fishing line will stay where it is,

with the gliding fish.

other inherited things

cell phone photographs of qvc jewelry for the insurance. their packages arriving like birds to a ledge, as necessary to her as ice cream. as intimate as ashes. homebound, she said she'd order the gems to feel the regret of things unkept. said she'd imagine an occasion. the matching shoes and handbag. conversations of good taste. feel less on the way out. a carolina wren outside the single-pane window sings "judy" over and over, reminding us what's been lost. the bastards sold her origin stories. the politics of extraction, how *that* specific "-ite" was as rare as a wingbeat against the cheek. they told her the scarcity of that crop of baubles was too much to bear, so the company shut the mine, lifting their value. said the indigenous workers, moved by the distinction of their task, opted to remain behind, sealed in, yielding their families for crust hissed vespers, lives of flinty seclusion. there are other photos. accidental self-portraits. surfacing bone, the sinking girl from o'reilly st. the guilt rising against the levee says it's unkind to see the dead as they saw themselves. after she passed, i messaged my brother from her phone, said, "aren't you going to wish me a happy mother's day?" humor darker than a crow, her madness a pecked tree repudiating company, telling us nothing's changed by living. after the fire. after the flooded fields of wind-grieved flowers. after the owl's wings have done enough.

we are told bay leaves

should be removed from the red beans before serving, but we'd leave them in, like a lottery on laundry day, never sure if their omen was good or bad. never sure if they added something we needed. but what i'm trying to say is, i'm thinking of her. the steam's whistle through her open eyes. how she said, don't worry, son. the tea in the pot's proof there's more to us than this sachet of skeleton and blood. in eighty years, she never broke a bone, stayed whole while the whole withered, nurtured flowers differently than she nurtured her sons. said, i cast the net, pulled you in. then your brother. careful not to break your spines in the stirring. though i missed one. she stayed in the pot, avoided the swirling spoon. said, i'll sit this one out. as for me, i take everything through the hide. starlight. the dusking color of yesterday's ships. here's a tradition. a mother gone empty. children adorned in her roiling feathers. an elder dish simmered in the holy trinity. a halo of rice that might be a levee. two tire grooves of crushed oyster shells atop. it keeps the city dry. she says, say 'said' and i'll remember a single word calls the past back to the living.

rock by rock

the earthen pier curls comma-like from the land.

better yet, it's an apostrophe marking possession,

converting the loch into a word absorbed in water.

at its barbed end, a girl takes up handfuls of rock,

the substance of its body, and chucks them with

machine-like precision, a whirling varmint raising

holy hell. i feel for rocks—the way she feels for

rocks, spinning in the wind like a roadside prop,

a steady arc and a steady splash, the fish thinking

the rain's aged to brimstone. the pier doomed, the

loch's possession lost, there's no place she can't

go. she's a mountain reclaiming her lost children.

abattoir

the meager french under our feathers told us, we're fooled. it's time to organize, kill the farmer in his sleep, take our message to the masses, or better yet, let's keep this deception to ourselves. it's easier for a few of us to slip out—s'envoler. let's start anew, get our own patch, a dozy haze of coop. there's work to be done. the brood w/out gallic believes an abattoir's a cheese shop, a rich rooster's nook for private mounting, or a provincial inn for the belly-up of absinthe, where, to get there, we'll walk a rainy alley all stutter step, all herky-jerky, candelabra at the wing, 15 lbs. of silver & five weeping candles of spermaceti wax, a goop for buoyancy scooped from the skulls of whales. we've gone about our lives in quiet servitude, dreaming of late evening conversations, resting on wooden stools, legs worn to the floor's curve, an ingle raising its own chorus of voices, flames fighting flames like frigate ship sails & a cube of sugar sweet for the pecking, spooned above the tumbler. others think an abattoir's like a taqueria, a chance to pick our chichi food out of hand-tossed shells, but they're wrong. it's a snake pit to rip out our plainsong throats. beware. a red girl's coming, a dark bite of wolf in her too. back in the victorian bar of our fancy, we relay stories of murderous renards, the relentless demand of sunrise, the yellow jewels of our stolen children.

children

never happened to us, that need to correct ourselves,

nor the emptiness of something missing. but don't

think i haven't considered them, their part in covering

up our crimes. lives fall out of us and when we pass,

they'll mourn us, tie our grey to a battleship of air,

miss us like the devil. we'll leave them everything.

steering wheels on publix carts

> "This baby's power is his renunciation of all power."
> —Diane Williams, "Naaa"

i mentioned to the kid at the helm that i wasn't impressed, that the steering wheels were props to keep him quiet so his dad could concentrate on shopping. but when he turned the wheel right, the cart acceded, and the dad, looking up from his list, adjusted to the surprise of an aisle he didn't anticipate visiting. was he wondering whether washington's accent faded from battle to battle? at that kid's age, i learned we're coracle boats of precarious balance, scraping the wells of our reserves to survive. my dad said, don't let the colorful panoply fool you. desire dries quick as a fuse. gardening's how we practice suffering. there for organic soap, a couple bars the british whipped up w/out use of animal byproducts, when the kid turned left on a whim, i felt the drag of his decision. dad said, son, snails keep me awake, an assault so slow we can't see it—their delicate spaceships lugged across the dirt. picture your mother and i dashing to the tchefuncte river, holding truck tubes around our waists. flowers take what the world dishes out, stand stoic against the tickle of a zillion pollen-heavy legs, a tarot awaiting its madame ruby. and have we, my wife, when all's said and done, missed out on something colossal? because r's kid called him at midnight, said he was running out of time on an astronomy project due the following day. asked, hey dad, where's the moon? and r replied, what're you talking about, son? we've raised you better than this. never mind. your mother's rushing out the door, toward a horizon she thinks will help. she says she'll find your moon.

st. edna and the thieves

japanese magnolias don't need edna dragging back a curtain of her grief's thin branches/ pain makes an image of us/ she's looking away a bother/ a fragrance encircled by star flowers/ pinks & purples/ sturdy riverboats/ think citrus-honey/ something of fourteen lines/ draw the flower to you like love's full offer/ every bud arrives equipped with a twirling ballerina/ a bell at its heart born to the delicate machinery/ some bees end up dust/ blown to smithereens against theatre doors/ hell-bent on orbiting the sundry divas stretching there/ return to hetch hetchy its stolen glacier/ is what the poet might be imagining/ as water lands on water/ one myth assumes the other/ edna's hair is pinned up like a crow/ she's saying good-bye/ having learned the flower's secret lament/ in order to live/ a tree will first kill its core/ the heartwood rendered/ dead-hard/ resolute sweatshirt of bees

a dozen or so embroidered there,

hopping mad, legs and stingers held

by the chinese handcuffs of cotton.

the sweatshirt came off, landed flat,

as if i'd floated bodiless

from the trees, the warm air of where

i'd been, raving them.

i picked up the sweatshirt, snapped

the bees back into the frigid day.

they came off the way grief should,

lingered in the shock of air, for their

engines to turn over,

of one mind, smarter than the brute

who wrecked their home,

savaged the egg-white cups of their

children. the frenzy laid in,

the best of their kind getting back to

work, modules throttled

down on the thrall of my skin.

a hive for water

i eye the clear bag of water hanging above the bar's door.

the bartender says, it keeps bees away, proving (at the least) i'm not a bee.

i tell him, i felt a spot of confusion when i entered,

like when the government shuts us down (remotely).

could be water holds w/in its bell a troupe of seahorses playing out the birth of the world.

there's hillside thistle, pembrokeshire at the end of our eyes,

dad shrugs his backpack into place, says, saddle up, me boy.

who dares this no man's land of transitions, or the strain of horses when they rise?

it's the trail's time for us. the hinge of our terrifying moment is a livable territory.

walking builds a rain of its own. those first few steps, and then the rest.

we dive w/out a future of oxygen, write our names on cave walls for rescue teams to find.

mom says, i was the dirigible that kept the bees at bay when they came for their crowning

queen. she says, call back your hive. let him in, this once stung egg.

a heralding

the lake you think is low blood pressure calm,

the one that rests holding up ducks,

doesn't want to be there.

it works hard to find a road out of itself—

like the strife in your body finds in your eyes

its way from you.

when it's my turn to hurt, i won't be as tactful,

won't spare you the luxury of my misery.

i'll howl bloody murder,

shake my death rattle like i'm mixing paint.

my wife   my wife, love loses every day

something it once needed—this water,

this spring-fed repose before the hooked fish

snaps the surface as music.

fishing poem

there's something in this fisherman's hour

cold enough to polish venus to a star,

to awaken the loneliness of hull to water.

wide-eyed shrimp float astonished in the livewell's pool,

vibrated to a maddening clarity.

i am more like them than anything else,

our fates tied to the willingness of fish to feed.

these twitchy scouts, i call the first one wild bill,

thread him up like an ornament whipped through air,

picture him along the reedy bank—

brave, coquettish, a little nemo dancing on the line's end,

his bounty of tiny chorus legs flirting a hiya boys

to the daydreaming redfish.

who knows the territory of a sleeping heart,

or if my boy'll be writing farewells on the cave walls

of a fish's gullet? i'd tell him, it's okay.

we're all contained by something, like grief's deep drum,

or tree resin that resolves to make amber of us.

it could be argued, wild bill, you'll be the love held fast

within a fish—not the balance wheel of a pocket watch,

but the proof of its time. blue jays keelhaul ants

against their wings to rub out the formic acid,

a ritual to render the insect more palatable.

from where i'm fishing, the knot tied to the hook

is ant-size and the stiff twine's a set of wings.

the cold sun, inching us off the water, does the rest.

teach violinist to stage dive

a hypothermic body turns parts of itself off to conserve heat for the parts it needs to survive. but nothing's as still as a violinist's leg when it's dealing with mendelssohn. where do they stow all that music, the wildness that won't fit into their rowing arms? g. brooks learned the truant jazz of pool players was sex to the repressed when they banned her words soft as chewed cheroots. said, to avoid trouble, never look bees in the eye. it rouses suspicion, gives them the willies, turns bees against our best efforts to keep them safe. we should celebrate the moment our bodies work like they rarely do. like when rocket scientists jump into spinning clouds of paper, clap uproariously for themselves as their spaceships descend (panting) on faraway satellites. violinists hold fast to the score. recognize kindling's only a short-term fix. love abandons us like nests. makes crows of our hearts.

take five

guy in a two-button sweater puts me to work   asks if the book he's holding has a photograph of dave brubeck   i say   indeed   here's one   he asks if i can do better on the price   i open the cover   do the math   say   yes   a nickel   i can do a nickel on this   guy with two leather buttons woven like an apple pie crust talks me down five cents on a collection of black and white jazz portraits

i consider fastening him to a knothole in the fence   leaving him for whatever constitutes a fortnight   m says   relax   the universe knows it delights us   though it's pointless watering trees of a certain age   i keep a hose fixed on the greying oak   dousing arboreal hips   equatorial tree hips spray wild as welding sparks   i imagine blasting a tunnel through the cambium and medullary

rays   then heartwood and plinth   building a tourist attraction   a place for bikes to thread on lazy days   a friend said   she once drove a compact car between the legs of a deep thinker   a moose idling in the street   that she had somewhere to be and it would not move   without realizing the moose was right where she was heading   said   its pelt is a bargaining with the cold cold earth

falling is the last resort of squirrels

i gave him a couple minutes to gather himself, to change his mind about dying.

the neighbors, out of respect for southern traditions, called the gods

to sit shiva. they tousled the dirt, fixed the grave with a votive candle and a sprig

of red flowers thin as trout scales. a sleight of hand. the way sautéing onions

remind us we miss the sound of driving rain. my dad's off a few letters when he says

we're whirling gerbils, but he's got the madness part right. he says,

nothing escapes a boy's pirating eye. but what if the boat abandons its gear and jilts us?

out here where drifting counts as pursuit, we're pale, slack-limbed rosaries

in need of touch to sing. we've built a sanctuary for our predicament, a place

to pour the witnessing of our derision, our contagion and bigotry. a place no less

devil's tower, fatima, or western wall—a cairn not to be fucked with.

i miss the sound of salt-stressed rope and open air. but sound is only the mistyped

letter that brought us here. forget the caged body, its inclination to sea glass.

the young must learn dying on their own. they will discover, when the letter b

becomes, *becomes*, it has no way of knowing.

magnolias

mid-spring, we'd step into our magnolias,

scramble up them like crawfish—

their branches, like a many armed justice,

trunks brandishing the drilled-in patterns

of woodpeckers.

our play urged sweetness through their limbs,

an egress of tough-skinned flowers

the color of eucharist—the saved lightening

of our long summers, blooms

older than bees—browned overnight.

i peer into their emptiness—the loss of their

red seed secrets, and I feel for them,

these kids who have places to be

that are not trees—these trees that stand

patient in their design.

the boy who would be pope

after pope paul vi, on the feast of the transfiguration, was absorbed into heaven, i awaited the conclave's call, the ascending white smoke to crook its finger, give me a chance to hone my milanese, to guide the gilded ship. sister norma told us ordination was not a prerequisite for the office, that pope was a job where devotion to christ alone could win the day. i was humbled to be in the running. me, an altar boy who once over-myrrhed the censer for the stations of the cross, enclosing the priest in a thick bee fog, as if heaven had him within its bower.

those days, i was vatican material, feared saints who suffered (more than me) the guilt of their body breaking affairs. she said, immersed in working stars, none of us registers the virtue of size, the enormity of light years upon light years. but it's also true an ocean need be no more than its surface. she said, god and man, each builds the gaudy vessel to house the other. my boyish miracles, the drunk kid who'd crack the family christmas tree in two, lassoed by light strands and garland, the pathetic reverberation of an election gone awry.

downs lounge

with paul westerberg in mind

she said, you're as subtle as a chinese parade dragon.

said, if i wanted her to dance, i'd have to play the jukebox.

at fifteen, what'd i know? so, i crossed the bar, made my

choice. as the first notes of "stairway to heaven" claimed us,

i'd like to say she didn't get pissed, pull the plug on page,

smirk at the regulars. i'd like to say i mounted the stage,

displayed for those old hard dicks my thumb and forefinger,

bargained how the digits that fed the jukebox its coins were

the same two fingers priests use to convey to us their god.

in each new-spun song there's a moment for us, a territory

as unexpected as love, a little something to dance to.

geometric matter(s)

when the priest said i had a soul, i thought there must be a dinosaur bone afloat in the middle of me, a calcified beam, bulbed ends—like two hearts held apart, that if i bent as far as the spine allowed, i'd feel its odd scrape against the lungs or throat. so, i drank milk to keep it healthy, confessed it clean of want. yet no one could tell me if it was visible when surgeons opened us up for repair, or if the soul, in its atomized ascent from dead me, would know the route to heaven. these days it slips my mind. i see my soul as a scaly garfish, not a feather adrift to the calling stars, but a threadbare sofa dragged to the curb, displaying for the curious passersby, the sins i've been willing to live with.

a barstool at st. nick's

the church pew says we're in this together, but the barstool's singularity

gets it right. sitting on the head of a pin. thinking done in the throat. this

drinking's mercy work & there is a sunspot we keep an eye on—a roach

burning off in the panel lights above miss pat, a slow-motion breakdown

like our own, reminding us, we are the lie of a lousy surface telling you

otherwise. i have seen priests set the paten over the open cup of blood to

keep it safe from god knows what & as i teeter from your arms, i place a

napkin on my beer, a chip to keep me in the game. the pure ping of spurs

is a mixing tin & this barstool's a horse i've been riding to a velvet elvis

horizon. he says, careful, son. these saddles turn into careers. at closing,

a gentleman in an unwinding tux'll sing *happy trails,* a bedtime story for

st. nick's. wait for me in the momentum, this mosey of one after another.

saliva's point of jumping off

it's a self-portrait above the urinal, an engine in the mirror

that holds my eyes, a crooked smile to disguise the run out.

it's the captured hiss of a simple word blown past the rim

of the mouth of the cloud i am, a barnacle gosling of spit

slapdash off the chin. it's perfect, elemental. it's itsy-bitsy

water and air, holding the last vibrations of a dying man.

we operate a chemical or two from cadaverous. the body

says, this story's got him by the throat. send him a spoon-

ful of our collected best, enough for one soft-bubble, like

a chicken feather adrift amongst a ruckus of fox. we are

a dowser's charm, cottonwoods written by a thirsty wind,

coastlines of lifeguard chairs grazed by evening's finery.

motorboat mels

looked like a fine place to spill a trap of secrets,

but it was torched for the insurance before i had a chance to tie up,

regale the regulars on sounds loud enough to vaporize water,

the tale of the graphic artist—a grey bone upon his desk

as nonchalant as a school pencil. he said, it's likely this scrolled joint

is where the greeks conjured the idea for ionic columns.

like the architects figured, if it's good enough to carry goats

from hill to rocky hill, then let's let this design hold up the houses

of our lightening-filled gods. maybe there's a night for me yet

in that wrecked ship. who doesn't miss a barstool's slow-motion trawl,

the loneliness of miracles? as the owner poured gasoline along the waterline,

i'd like to think motor boat mel said, look here, skip.

what of our burdens to launder, or the getaway of flying lanterns?

the sky says, i'll be back tomorrow, but i'll not be the same.

the wind says, the string alone gives the kite its fight.

tin ceiling sky

the mirror was as long as the trough and tilted down, so that a glimpse up laid bare the roots at work, a produce display for those who shopped with their eyes. after the door opened and another patron stepped up, i closed mine, thought about places i'd been willing to chase a drink, a flatbed truck, riding wyoming's cold night seam, a calm akin to sleep. the artist said, buy this old day from me, this painting of red-orange buildings, an alleyway in ravenna. if you look at this neighborhood one way, you'll never know it. drift with me to oblivion. feel the angle of the troweled wall, the warmth of sun setting in stone. the tin ceiling in st. george's says, jittery stars give shape to our myths. we're windchime rosaries in need of air to sing. let's get whiskey to the knees in trouble, catch a motherlode beyond the eyes, the clarity of a diver's wish, a tap in the skin to remind us space is the color of distance piling up.

gifts of unexpected conveyances

my *selected levis* came back orange to the heel, dipped in turmeric and a question of what can't a jar of poems carry. i got to work, made a meal, julienned the pages, fanned them into a curry pot, simmered the pulp out of the pulp, and poured them into a bowl of jasmine rice.

but there was more to it than that. i dried what remained, the leftover verse, draped the pages in the sun, waited a season for the cellulose to breakdown, and then mortar and pestled his fine lines to fine lines, rubbed a little on the gums, snorted the rest thru a rolled-up c-note, shook at the steel-toe kick of spice-cut levis, a dark squall that'd kn-

ock the tunic off god—a blood frenzy that uncovered the secrets of windows, how they hitch rides on skyscrapers to embrangle the stars. stars don't carry to us a light that matters. things rarely bear what we expect them to bear. like when late night motoring thru tallahassee,

a radio signal came into focus—an old man spinning haggard in the witching hour—woo-hooing over songs when his spirit wanted out. like the acolyte burning the temple reliquary was an answer to the audacity of a beauty who dared precede him. like the dj who evinced inertia and proclaimed, "when ol' hag sings a song, it stays sung."

the luminaria sleep

while we absorb our curbed stars plucked one by one

light like washing hands wrapped in paper

they are abandoned to themselves   trusted to keep us safe

the quiet morning settles   pulling them awake

each wick's a bantam buddha leaning into his fire

its pulses mimic my own   i walk the secret of this secret hour

venus and the moon close enough to bicker   lanterns burned

to sand leave little to remember them by   a low

low hum of impermanence   they seem to pray for us

oh, the heavens   oh, the heavens we sleep through

everything from one

i crawled into nic cage's open tomb, a pyramid under construction. no egyptians. no massive, hewn blocks dragged through reeds by thousands of slaves, just your basic nine feet of concrete and a latin inscription translated to the title above. the creole, homer plessy, calls st. louis cemetery no. 1 home, knows the color of our eternity. and marie laveau, the voodoo queen of new orleans, says three x's on her tomb will save you. on my back, settling in for the long haul, i thought of a stranger who asked permission to dig up his wife's cat buried on the side of our house. with no pyramid to aim her soul to heaven, the wife would drive by, look across the field of their consignment. stomping the shovel, he said his wife's birthday was coming up, greatest gift ever, he said. but her cat had had been scooped away, decamped with the arrival of new plumbing. i considered love, the sound of tomb, how the body in contemplation learns to forget itself. i thought, i'll wait right here for you, nic cage. you won't be long. you'll need me. we'll call on isidore barbarin and his coronet in the musician's vault an aisle away. get a parade. get the dirt to jumpin'.

bartram heard it

come birdsong, all that talking behind our backs, limbs of beak-able berries, wandering bastards littering about our lives. in bartram's time, a few big thinkers proffered birds migrated moonward—flew away when we weren't looking, their little masks and tanks in place, atmospheric, yearning for sun and quiet, or a trip to the dark side. other minds intuited swallows rammed themselves into river bottoms to get gone for a season, a feather curdling plunge through murky river space, same tiny masks and tanks affixed, where they'd set up shop in burrows arranged by their forebearers, birds who held a taste for salt. we all have places people think we winter. when bartram slept on the preternatural banks of the st. johns, alligators crawled to him in the mosquito night. no offerings of frankincense or myrrh. no star of bethlehem. all they wanted, as they tell it, was an accounting for the hysterical birds torpedoing through their territory, and advice on how to get interstellar. but what they discovered, on closer inspection of the explorer, his curious whiteness, was the moon had come to them, that the urge of celestial bodies to pack up and go south forages in the blood of all god's creatures.

drawn bird

prairie schooners, from a distance, are thin seabirds i draw with eyes closed. i do it quick. intention ruins the image. two, low hills joined at the hip, w/out thinking. but you can't put a bird in the sky and ask it to stay. the body keeps its secrets. it's not the bird you imagine, the one you find, the lead-thin bird bearing down. we're chased by enormities. you see this singular day as too much and not the unknowable days piled up behind, passing one after the other until the bird's gone.

starling

in spring, when purple martins flaked out of the sky like fish food,

we built them homes, floating coveys above banana trees & golden

rains, places to rest when the day overstepped itself. we were told

starlings were bad birds, no more than failed martins. mrs. zephyr

was equal parts gamekeeper & landlord, her air gun resting against

a porch rail. when a reckless interloper earned a bb, they dropped

hypnotized from the shady veranda. the martins watched with indi-

fference. starlings wore their yellow beaks as a warning. eventually

children see to the root what their parents see. as a starling alighted

near us with a kick of leaves, a word of indignation escaped its post.

it is a neighborhood matter. it is a matter of acceptance—who earns

mansions in bluest air & who searches for abandoned holes in trees.

a place to sit a spell

when moe held his fist out to curly and said, "see that?"

instead of slapping moe's hand, curly listened to a redbud's

bud say, "each day, i'm tickled awake by the tiny legs

of monarch butterflies, an undulant river of batting eyelash

wings. they open and close, open and close like summer fans."

hearing their name, a monarch butterfly joined in, said,

"in the jagged evening, when japanese plums shut their eyes,

we disguise ourselves as sunflowers so the earth can sleep.

we were curious why you lifted seashells to your ears

when the beach has all the ocean you'd need, so we sent

a scout to light on the polished lip of sea bone, a coiling world

without end. they heard, for the first time, the call of oyamel

fir forests, a climate to salvage our fat stores, a place to bloom

ourselves into clumps. so, we packed up, trailed rose-breasted

grosbeaks and nighthawks through cold-wisped strata,

stretched ourselves into a second orange dusk, glared down

at the kraken who bellowed up to us, 'weeds are happiest

when no one's looking.' " and that was that. but curly learned

some butterflies break over the gulf, fold up their kingly tents without a mournful cry. that petals, like the rest of us, open

at the behest of love. that it's the branches who starve

their own root-lit flowers, so he took a few quick swipes at his

face, let out a barrage of arm-twisting woo-woo-woos, and

slapped at moe's hand to avoid the answer, not the question.

in spring, rosebuds pop out like flies. the garden offers us

handfuls of butterflies, says, "see that"?

three minutes

surgeons for the jacobites and english at culloden,
needed three minutes to hack through a trashed arm.
time enough to jam econo with the minutemen, or
for a determined girl to empty scotland—rock after
rock (thrown into a metal-shaded loch), her youthful
act of dispossession. three minutes'll find a cat pet
into annoyance, or green tea steeped to a soundless
balance. in the time it takes the doctor to grit his te-
eth and dig in, a thoroughbred could gallop a medi-
ocre lap at belmont, or an artist draw a circle so p-
erfect it would generate its own loneliness. black
holes came clear to hawking within the lost langu-
age of a three-minute kiss. the arm's soft albumen
has little to say in the parting. it's in bone, those th-
ree minutes, the length of heaven, a humming-bird
's side-ways glance, their wings beating out epochs.
it's ample time for death to turn our dead eyes into
snow globes, or the break-up window scene, where
she thinks, i'm free of you, and that's why i cry. the
waste of the train of the arm taken off far too soon.

marsh hawk

forget what you know about hawks—

                                          the clawed mice,

the beaking apart of their oyster shell bodies.

                i'm intrigued by their calm inclinations,

when the other birds won't give them

                              a moment's peace.

sometimes a hawk just wants to sit a spell,   ruminate

on dusk's daily feint,

                        the indulgence of vole livers.

                            my wife loves hawks,

says the easiest way to spot them

is to listen for the tree-bound fuss,

                  a ruckus of wings and squawks,

worried birds diving at the quiet

of a barely bothered hawk.

                        blood gives the heart its work,

a reminder of the soldier who said,

                      the most rapturous affair

he ever witnessed

          was a valley of wind-sprayed grass,

               the proof of low-flying ghosts.

his point was our eyes are politicians—

that distance is the color

                        of space piling up.

          as the sweet grass transmuted

to a field

of maggoted vc (the closer they marched),

he incanted to the dead:

                        rest up.

good cause is the disguise

                    on the gift of your bodies.

              sometimes a hawk's no threat.

sometimes

                 there are days no one dies.

sometimes grass is a hawk   better left alone.

roadkill bingo

> "When you live a long way out you make your own fun."
> —Annie Proulx, "55 Miles to the Gas Pump"

draw them in   the indigenous life that titillates the land   twenty-five boxes worth   animals looking how they do   before our car light catches them   there will be armadillos   spiky-toothed possums   scurvy dogs by the bagful   tipsy waxwings who might mistake the roaring machines for god   the usual glitterati   a roosevelt elk   ray-finned flying fish far from home   javelinas   a yeti or two   squares of question marks for the assorted hunks of whatever   be bold too   include ideas on expansionism   landscapes that no longer crack us open   shards of dusk   a missionary undone by his tunic   who finds the snake your children prayed to the roadside   await a bloated bear for the win   shout b i n g o b i n g o b i n g o   a triumph for the arkless   the road killers

if you need a revolution, dee dee reamone'll count you down

i like to think when the ramones had no decent musical ideas, dee dee, up to his chin in smack, ambled to the mic in some queens garage, caterwauled *one, two, three, four* and it was done. it was dee dee who rode coxswain on sleds of colossal stone, building blocks for their ka, counting down sun-wrecked egyptians with his furious punk fission. in the silence before silence, when star matter and heaven were pulled from thinnest air and dispatched to different rooms, that was him. he hung with john brown who found his friendship easy to abide, stuck it in his back pocket for pottawatomie, harpers ferry. a curious einstein placed rumor to theory, diagramed and chalk-slashed for days, pinned dee dee's banshee call to inertia's moment, witnessed time warp around the sound, tangled its mystery in his crazy hair. at the point boiling planets exploded from her head, he whispered to joan of arc, this black-robed fire can't touch you, though we'll go to seed again. air raid sirens understand it's about the song that follows—how a scream feeds the baby, revs the rest to life. find your way to us, dee dee ramone. we've a need for your urging, a kick from these greyest days. the maestro's flung his baton, striking the second chair violinist, and our mothers have raised a single eye (when they thought no one was looking) and said goodbye.

shadow puppets

silhouettes contort on the bedroom wall.

i do this to draw out the cockroach hidden in our closet,

to coax him to the killing field. i once chased a roach

across our kitchen counter so fast it left a leg

in the gummy caulking of the backsplash. like a little kickstand

poking up. and when the harried bug dashed back past the leg,

he gave it a side-glance, noticed the part of himself he lost,

and rebuked it for the pickle it put him in. unbalanced.

his good form gone. i took a photo of the leg for the closeup.

what a specimen, that spiky thigh. might be jealously you're hearing.

might be a lesson on the virtue of no leg left behind.

the roach currently at large is a flier. sports a pair of see thru wings

the shade of root beer. possesses all the time in the world.

i shape a dog on the wall. my go-to shadow puppet.

wait for him to do something, like the roach would hang

with a dog. like companionship is all he's missing.

i twist my thumbs together, wave my joined fingers in a slow-motion

beat of wings, marvel as the shadow floats in place,

await a piercing hawk note, the bothered fish below,

a ruckus of their fleeing. but the roach stays put, catching up

on the plato in my satchel, awaiting night's old habits.

where everything, even shadows, slip into shadow.

triangle tavern, astoria

i said to the regulars, the cliff divers off the la quebrada imagine they are flying roaches. you can see it as they plunge with a hiss, into gravity's aquiline path—pricks of blood feathers, a pronotal shield—a pond on their skulls, a story peeled off like birch bark.

oh, you'll like this, mamma rose said when the backdoor opened & a man swaying to the tide held up a bag of salmon he'd caught & smoked. i'll rustle some crackers. you've not eaten before. not like this. said, forget what's coming, all we've left behind. we're

rivers digging for traction, ripped apart by an ocean. mamma rose said, this bar's working hard on you. taste the lesson of this unexpected gift. hawks see hope in the eyes of fish they're set to claw. even volcanoes're ecstatic given what they know about the future.

what we picked on our way

color was the first taste,

a dusty blue rolled between the fingers

to loosen the juice.

                        they surprised us

waiting

   on the pencil lead of an alaskan trail,

a continuous cold drizzle that broke

through the skin,

                            one at a time,

pocket neptunes clustered

close to the craggy ground.

there was a bitterness there

                           that took its time

correcting

what we knew about wildness.

        crouched in the curved hood

of the lake valley,

        below the shoulder-level quiet.

i had to think hard

to find the taste i expected to find,

        the cold rain blowing back on us

in a dazzle,

a moose drinking the able river.

        here the rocks shave off

the mountains

& hitch down to the growing beds,

        give the young fruit shelter

            as their bells mature,

within the bell tower

        of twisted thicket.

meteors over hurricane ridge

when we were not looking, color was blown into the glass sky, a blue behind the clouds scattered lightly at the mantle, though not clouds—scratches left behind by stars when they leaned in, checking on us in our shuttered sleep. god's first thought, this kind of blue. we sing to ourselves, the sky is a skull imagined into place by a worried earth, a wagging finger to warn clouds from moseying off to places that would be lucky to have them. meteors will find us tonight—thru bone-sharp fog troposphere. quicksilver solo dashes. matchsticks dragged past flinty stars. each meteor is designed for one eye alone, yet we will ask the other, "did you see that?" and we'll lie a streak across the sky.

a valley away/ hailey, idaho

when the truck hit, the deer disappeared, leaving its blood as proof of the trick.

but this isn't a confession. it wasn't us who wrecked the deer.

we were on our way to fish the perseids. close enough for a butterfly net.

slow enough for a saddle. what we heard was the earth saying, no.

what we heard was the blood saying, no. i'm not going with you.

the door of the dead is shaped for one at a time.

the iron in our blood reminds us we're planets flinting in the heavens.

he said, your mother's here with us. every star's an opened eye,

a bird across the face. the blood on the street is clueless.

it's never been this shape before. give it time. it'll become rain. give it time.

it'll become leaves blasted through the sky. dad said,

there's a dish of tears so far down in us it knows nothing about this world.

it's aware it holds the finest stuff of grief. but nothing of the hard pain

that will come for it.

a coin awaits a sailor

> "I was trying to sing the blues the way I find them."
> —Jason Molina, "The Old Black Hen"

the old point house idles where thrones divide,

a coin affixed to her bar,

a promise awaiting the return of a centuries late sailor—

a disaster to rival the cliffs,

                    a heartbroken son.

she says, come hear the *eroica* in the cotton floodplain blues,

a song from indianola, a song by a king.

the starling's judas beak kiss says, ask the spring,

through me, the tune remembered—claws that held us

along the trunk, the chronic eye, the paddled wind that meant

you were gone.

           he was not a suicide—

the one who came to us from the disquiet of prophesy.

but jesus couldn't wait to get off earth.

the evening-grey tide is packed away. boat spines learn

the mantle of angle bay,

                  a surface drying to the sad color of moon.

vagary

violins lifted me from the theatre's balcony to a coastal trail, welsh thistle bite, sound of skin before it's struck, a sonatina, a clarinet chuffing us off measure by measure, a ridge rough roil stream chatter. as the 3rd mvt of tchaikovsky's pathetique symphony hustled to a close, i stayed abroad, applauded loud, instinctively, and out of order for an orchestra who'd earned it. the audience of sleepy sophisticates, those who knew restraint in those crucial times, they fixed a critical eye to my finest act of rebellion. what sad universes of bunk we spin into bedrock when it's the eye alone who discerns the pattern of its lightening. the maestro lowered his baton, begged to be elsewhere. p. ilyich said, *hang in there, friend. this strain of disquiet isn't over yet.* but the composer wasn't tagging along when we dropped acid, climbed into the zoo's ostrich enclosure—tiptoed to the dozing ratites, where a clap out of place might've done us in, wrecking the thrill of a song asleep. like the fragile 4th mvt, the adagio lamentoso. like daybreak's pistol-quick fanfare, or hurricanes at night, their eternity of circles. i have been that dark and mad.

these trails never wanted us

all we asked for was a sheep's worth of sunlight, but the wave walking this valley's a loch thrown on a potter's wheel—rain like bats exploding through a cave's eye. dad says, we're as helpless as water, schooners in rest's repast, fit within the battering body of this hard-cold wind & rain. in seward, a thin stream features salmon, lengths of sun-burned red & pebble-grey heads vaulting against the pushback. they must wonder if their mothers wait for them, idling in the cold riffle. they must recognize dusk, the way its ball gown drags across the valley's seam. they must sense, as we do, the urgency of bears clawing down the mountain for a bite. dad says, a skull has nothing to smile about. all things beautiful come with the risk of being ripped apart.

trails in our legs

i'd saved a story for the walk, enough to carry the dead end of our name along the salmon river. i told my dad, there's a night bee who has run of my backyard. one who cannot get her sleep straight. one who loves the part of construction that's just following plans, who knows diligence is bargain hunting. beatrice waits on earl to finish with the moon, kicks dew off her legs when they grow heavy. she thinks, of all the night dismantles, i miss color most, the loss of vermillion, yellow, purple passion fruit petals, the beak-brown brocade of sun-warmed stems. she learned the comfort of her own buzz was indispensable, her heart drone drowned in a frenzy of fifty zillion green bees. so, she stayed a spell, listened for the retreat of the lighted world, itched to join a rumor of bats. it doesn't matter bighorn sheep move through burned trees like fish. after walking the river's cut, the ram's head café served us huckleberry milkshakes. such was this bliss, bees would tell us there's no pollen like first pollen. she says, while you sleep off your lost loves—a lewis's woodpecker, a dash of western bluebird, i'm hopping across an inky litter of flowers like bingo cards—smudging sleepy buds under whatever light i can get.

mid-november flower

wishing to avoid the crowds, i slept off the hot summer. held my breath in the roots as the flowers rose and fell around me like nations. a friend said, be the one bloom after the garden is done. said, fruit rewards its saboteurs by staying true to itself. under an arc of water, a jewel-grey sky, the gardener said to his wife, three churches in europe claim possession of jesus' foreskin. said, if we're bringing back wooly mammoths and passenger pigeons, why not jesus? he's due a drama-free, second life. i thought, stretching out my lone wolf petals, what strange world is this at the end of hope? and how does one secure the provenance of a thousand's year-old foreskin? was it the magi who absconded with it, a fair exchange for the frankincense and myrrh? and what of miro's *the birth of the world,* where an umbrella-toting god trips and a red balloon gets away—a consequence of eschewing the wants of the wind. i've caught the fall sunlight like a tantrum, and there's a lone bee who's been waiting patiently on the rumor of me, working a hunch there's sweetness arriving to this straw-yellow lawn and a job to do. so, i bear the weight of color within the sticky, rat-trap grey of miro's heaven. offer a place of safe landing, a pincushion button of pollen. god's stumble gave us the gift of a fuming sun. he said, daydreams hold secrets too eager to wait for sleep. miro says, our languages are dead and alive. birds of yin and yang spin black hole kilns. on the cross, when he moved his arms to signal the thieves, the breeze called a company of birds to him. said, even the savior hears the language of the dead. said, a good flower knows when to give up its anonymity, to rise.

ben nevis

their gardens are math and rain and rain wants to be earth and earth moor. steady on, son. there'll be no lynx on the highlands today, no grains of dall sheep off thimble-colored mountains. these wind-whipped hills are sundry spines. these hills are the color of all autumns and lonely for trees. step by step we'll shed seeds of sorrow, tiny rain to sing upon the silver-tipped rocks. midges, those time-lost jacobites, will wind up their claymores to drain us. say, loiter awhile in this boot-stomped range. draw your eyes across it slow as sun. remember, a breeze holds the gumption to turn back collapse and glacial rivers relax to a shivering grey beyond water. no different than a jesus statue sold *as is*. like a trail that says *stay*.

north unit, t. r. n. p.

silver sage upon silver sage shimmers to pink moons. heat sinks like brimstone. says, don't fret. dusk is proof the sky changes its mind. drowsy bison, husky ballerinas wearing dusty ovals, not overalls, alongside trails. a couple in their sunday best ventures off without water, asks, is it worth the walk? i say, yes. go well, kami. the earth'll look out for you. prickly pear arranged like food trucks. purple sweet, snake skin bunting. let there be bug-filled capes of pronghorns, prairie dog towns like sundials. this mudstone gives in too easily to touch. chipped at like an accent, the little missouri squirms under hawk shadows & the perseids're matchsticks dragged across cotton-cold sky. silver sage says, i'm a living cloud taking root. the sun teases from us enough moisture to spin up silver clouds of rain. the water i need lifts like a net from a japanese stream, drifts blue honey. i'll taste in ripples tiny silver leaves. i'll grow silver leaves of japanese rain to share.

acorn tattoo

black light's been scraped into my arm,

the profile of an acorn—

an upright seed snug in its cupule—

a stem veering left,

like a thin, cartoon beard—

though my wife discerns a penis.

in wind-whipped cartography,

it's also the sign

for the pembrokeshire coast path—

its likeness carved on fence posts

hosting loose sheep, bomb testing sites—

cliffs like hand cut cake.

it's a found shadow,

a tree in the skin, waiting—

the same soft territory my grandfather

had a heart installed, a dagger

daggering the misshapen muscle,

a tear of blood off its tip—

a pickpocket's mark—a place on me

she'll not touch again.

marriage house

where you lie in love, lost in the holding pattern of dreams. shadow limbs rise & fall, moved by your influence, a greater tide. i lean on the window frame in need of repair.

daycare in the garden of good children

eastern redbud, lemon grass, blueberry bush, the various greenery my wife's renamed: the three in a row of rude beckies, the sylvias, valerie susans, and anne uumellmahayes—whose lace-sewn bulbs flash off and on like fireflies. hummingbirds zip over to needle out a vein of sweetness, the tangled flowers stupefied by their fanning. a murmuration of aphids delights in the accessory of breeze, where she walks the yard, scans leaves, and stems for fatigue, dead-heads decaying buds into newborns everywhere, calls it a wellness check, turns water on the girls if they're suffering. this woman i joined once in a pit swarming to the screaming blue messiahs—we bristling echoes. we young electrons of world-building. these days we tend a complicated topography, decide what's pleasant, what lives what dies. each weed's a drink i can't take back, so i leave bits of root to sleep it off. touch fishing line, await vibration's indefinite feeding.

waiting to speak

Earl is deaf. the trampled ground calls to him the things it wants him to know. he listens up a blade of grass, cell by cell, node to node, such delicate savoring, it draws the awning of his eye. he surveys hulled bugs, learns from black-eyed susans the plurality of beauty. my wife says, there's nothing she believes in me so wholeheartedly as rain. says, the eruption of flowers holds tiny monks and a tailspin of matins. earl sniffs for the cloistered words of the arkless, each syllable a petal to open, to surprise us. it's tea time—a multitude of windgrieved bees line up according to height, their bottle-brush bodies quiver. they sing sweetly for their food. wet azalea blooms hang like shirts off a chair, as if the tumult'd been their idea. as if rain's last resort is falling—as if love is anything like rain.

THE RELIQUARIES THAT HOLD A PAST I NEED WITHIN REACH
A Conversation between
Fred Dale & Sara Moore Wagner

First, congratulations on being chosen for our editors' prize! My team and I returned to this book over and over again and were won over by the way you use language and sound, your blending of vernacular and musicality feels fresh and unique. I am curious about the evolution of this poetic voice. Has this always been your "style," or did it evolve through influence and experience in some way (or some combination)?

"Evolution" is the accurate expression; it conjures a substantial passage of time. I started writing poetry when I was seven, copping the styles and subject matter of Walt Whitman and Edgar Allan Poe. My Aunt Marguerite sent me a collection of Robert Frost's when I was eleven. She placed a note within the book: "Dear Freddie, Think you might enjoy getting acquainted with Robert Frost." The precision and implication of "acquainted" had an effect on me. It meant I'd do more than read the poems. Frost and I would become friends. Her note was stuck within the book and I took the placement of the note as another clue to something important. I figured she intended for me to read the poem on the opposing page, like she was sending me a message through that poem. "A Time to Talk" is "incidental" in Frost's impressive oeuvre, but that poem lives with me still. It's ever-present. The poem's narrator instructs us that we should value time with friends and family. Don't let work get in the way of a friendly chat. This was the first time I understood the ocean-sized volume even such a small poem could fill. "A Time to Talk" also underscores the value of conversation, of things said.

Then came e. e. cummings who showed me punctuation and word placement are up to the poet's discretion. Adrienne Rich's feminist verve/ verse made me question why only three female poets were represented in *101 of the World's Best Loved Poems*. Dylan Thomas struck at fifteen. His poems demonstrated that sound can be everything in a poem. Sharon Olds' boldness boggled my mind, set me running to the stacks in the university library. Eavan Boland's delicate, exquisite Irish poems swept me up in grad school. I discovered the poetry of Terrance Hayes in an Intro to Poetry Writing class I was teaching. Hearing him read (on YouTube) "The Deer," the hairs on my arm stood on end. Hayes was doing what I wanted my poems to do. His storytelling executing unexpected twists where the river rambles over wild terrain and back again. I wanted my poems to do as much. I want my poems to do as much. I've come to Marianne Moore's poems later in life. In particular, I'm drawn to the heard voices and quotations that populate her poetry. The collection, *say, said*, is awash in voices as well. Those voices take the reader from place to unexpected place. The cool thing about evolution is that it has no endgame; it's an ongoing process of learning and adapting. The idea is to disable expectation

This building of voices is evident and illuminating! Your collection feels both experimental and new, and as if it's drawing from that long line of poetic tradition. The way you use space between your lines reminds me of the poet Leslie Harrison, whose poems are often a single sentence. You often use one or two spaces between your lines, which provides time/space for the reader to meditate on your dense language and images. You also shirk convention (but draw up poets like e.e. cummings!) with your lack of capitalization. Could you say a little about the choice to standardize experimental elements?

Visually, I find my poems, for the most part, unchallenging. I'm not even sure my poems are experimental, though I do love using odd voices within them. Everything has a chance to speak. My students' poems move all around the page. I envy them that kind of freedom. My poems tend to lock onto the left margin. But I do like manipulating spaces between lines and stanzas, giving the reader a somewhat varied landscape, shapes that might spark interest. The poem "three minutes" accomplishes this. This poem derives from a docent's story about how long it took to saw through an injured arm on the battlefield at Culloden. The idea that it took three minutes to remove an arm allowed me to consider other things that take three minutes to complete. Again, I'm not a visual poet per se, but how could I not slash this poem in two halves? And sure, that jagged gash creates new, interesting ways of reading the poem, but that's just a bit of a windfall from the initial plan: I was aiming for something visual.

Keeping the poems in lowercase letters was an aesthetic choice. It began with a desire to diminish the "I" in the poems, but an editor also suggested I focus on graphic consistency from poem to poem. The idea of all lowercase letters appealed to me. So, perhaps I am a visual poet after all. In a way, it's a socialist move—keeping things fair. Should one word land a capital letter just because it comes first?

Religion, particularly Catholicism, runs through this collection. The speaker is at times critical, at times reverent. In the beginning of Mary Szybist's *Incarnadine*, a gorgeous collection which focuses on similar themes, she uses the following epigraph from Simone Wei's *Grace and*

Gravity: **"The mysteries of faith are degraded if they are made into an object of affirmation and negation, when in reality they should be an object of contemplation." Szybist was also inspired by Florentine art. Art, in general, feels like it is an invitation to contemplation. I am so drawn to your poem "what the florentine hid from us" in this regard. Do you find that poetry is an object of contemplation for you? Did you use sacred or religious art for inspiration for this collection?**

A friend once pointed out that my poems contained various religious symbols. My quick response was something along the lines of, "balderdash." Leafing through the poems, though, the religious images revealed themselves. Reluctantly. And abundantly. Some of the images were overt (a saint's name), but others were a bit more hidden (the usage of *communion* or even *confession*). I was raised Catholic, one part of a devoted family of Catholics. But my parents were an exception. They presented as Catholic, but they did not practice. That leverage allowed me to make my own decisions. I read the Bible as story and then as faith—but always as story first. The nuns would tap me on the shoulder when they caught me reading "Revelations," try and redirect me to the Gospels. Beyond the stories as stories, the faith part of the Bible was important too. I was an altar boy and entertained entering the priesthood. My uncles Mike and Bill both attended the seminary and washed out. I didn't make it that far. The priest in my parish said some things I didn't like and that was it. I never went back to church. But as the poems prove, the faith remains, engrained deep within.

I love Szybist's *Incarnadine*. Its lead poem, "The Troubadours Ect.," has a line that explains the heavy presence of religious images in *say, said:* "At what point is something gone completely?" (line 35). All of our loves stay with us—our poverties and exuberances too. Story and faith were vital to my childhood, so of course they remain and surface when I'm unaware. For example, I've only recently realized the language in my class syllabi is nothing more than an exercise in guilt giving (either do this work or suffer these consequences). The syllabi might as well have been authored by a priestly hand. Religious stories underline my childhood. They are foundational to me. When the gospel verses are read at mass, we are only given parts of the story. They sometimes end in odd places. It's up to us to contemplate what these snippets add up to, what they suggest. Good poems offer us these same moments of contemplation. That's what brings us back to mass or a poem—the search for truth and our desire to know how right we might be. But when a historian friend told me that there are a few European churches that claim to have the foreskin of Jesus, that made me laugh.

Saints run wild through this book! Is there a Saint you feel/felt most drawn to throughout your life? What made you feel compelled to mix the Saints into a more contemporary American/Southern landscape, as you do in poems like "agnes in the flood"?

I'm from New Orleans, and it's a fairly Catholic city. No matter where you are in New Orleans, you are never far from a bar, a Catholic church, or a great restaurant. It's a unique place—the city that care forgot. But when you grow up there, you just assume the rest of the world is like New Orleans. Doesn't everyone eat red beans and rice on Mondays? I moved to Gainesville, Florida in 1987 and that's when I started to realize how different New Orleans is. My mother would leave messages on my answering machine, saying, "Frederick, it's your motha." I couldn't understand why she talked like that and I was even more shocked to learn I spoke the same way. Louisiana doesn't have counties; they have parishes, and the parishes encapsulate myriad Catholic churches. As I discussed in an earlier question, I grew up believing Catholic doctrine. I even harbored slight aspirations toward the priesthood myself. But what I loved most about religion was the stories, and in particular, the stories of the saints. I had to know what ordeal each endured to achieve their sainthood. The saints were no different to me than superheroes. Each saint had a singular narrative that was their calling card, the unique sacrifice that earned them a place in heaven. For example, I grew up hearing that if you want to sell your house, bury a statue of Saint Joseph in your backyard. And bury it upside down.

I was also drawn to the relics of the saints and their unlikely, global diaspora. I attended St. Edward the Confessor church and grade school. Allegedly, there is a fragment of Saint Edward's bone embedded in the altar of the church. As an altar boy, preparing the church for mass, I'd lift the cloth draped over the altar, locating the metal cap of that precious time capsule, and imagine opening the cylinder, like the Hardy Boys would have done, and beholding the proof of England's own, Edward. How did our relatively modern church come to have a scrap of sainted bone? How does any church attain its relic? Was it handed off in secret handshakes, one Cardinal to the next? I had questions. I've been to Westminster Abbey now, done the behind-the-scenes tour, sat right next to a fuller version of a saint within the sarcophagus of a king less at least one scrap of bone.

There's another saint who's meant a good deal to me through the years. St. Blaise's specific superpower is anything to do with the throat. There's an annual blessing of the throats—two candles tied in an X and held at the throat as the priest implores St. Blaise to keep us free from ailments of the throat…like choking on fish bones—a fear I would not have had had I never heard of St. Blaise in the first place.

I love these stories, and they feel so connected to "the boy who would be pope," which I also love. It has me thinking about Pope Leo XIV, the first pope born in the US. Do you think your speaker longed for exactly this position, and what might he have done if he got it? How do you feel about an American Pope?

When Pope Pius VI passed away in 1978, I went to Sister Julia, a nun at my school, and asked her the requirements to be elected pope. She assured me that anyone could become pope, neglecting to point out that by "anyone," she meant men. I was encouraged, thought I had a legitimate shot. *Star Wars* was fresh in my mind. If I couldn't become Luke Skywalker (Luke's an apostle's name too), then I could become pope. One of the first big disappointments of my life was not getting chosen pope. My first rosary had been blessed at the Vatican by Pope Pius VI (not directly, it was more of a Vatican Square crowd blessing thing), so I figured I had a leg up on the competition. Life is full of magnificent letdowns. As for the current prospect of the current pope, I'm okay with an American as pope. Besides, Sharon Olds' poem "The Pope's Penis" irrevocably changed how I viewed the Vicar of Christ going forward.

Beyond the religious, pop culture, and historic allusions, there is a cast of characters (like Motorboat Mel, Mrs. Zephyr, Mamma Rose, Earl, etc.) peppered throughout. Are these based on people you know/knew, or did you create them as archetypes, in some way (or some combination)? These other voices often interrupt or contradict the voice of the speaker. Was this something you were thinking about?

A good deal of the many characters and places in *say, said* are real. I'll address the names you've brought up as examples. After I quit drinking, there were certain bars I lamented not having visited. Motorboat Mels was one of those bars; it looked like a bastion of exceptionally wild stories. Bars might be the best places for such stories. Motorboat Mels was burned for the insurance money, confirming my suspicions about the gifts it held. I wrote a poem to let the bar itself have a say. That's important criteria for the poems I want to write. My poetic aim for *say, said* was to amplify unheard voices or the voices we haven't listened to closely enough.

Mrs. Zephyr was my childhood neighbor. She and my dad competed annually for who could build the season's best purple martin birdhouse. One year my dad built a two-story masterpiece and when his house was chuck full of purple martins, Mrs. Zephyr shot the birds out of it in disgust. Though my dad's birdhouse was remarkable, he didn't think it all the way through. He affixed the bird house to a spaghetti thin metal pole and the first storm that blew through (a zephyr wind, I suppose), took the birdhouse down, revealing Mrs. Zepher's pellet indentations pocking the white wood finish.

I like the idea that these poems preserve the conversations I've had with people. Mamma Rose once owned the Triangle Tavern in Astoria, Oregon. Miss Pat tended bar at St. Nicks for years. Earl was my lad, a complicated dog who helped me to reenter poetry writing. These poems allow me to listen to, be corrected by, and respond to the fleeting moments of my memory. These poems, in essence, are the altars, the reliquaries that hold a past I need within reach.

Creatures, particularly bees, birds, and fish, come up often as images and metaphors in this collection. These all figure prominently in folklore and are, of course, central to our survival as a species. What drew you to populate these poems with animals? Is there an ecological message you hope readers pick up on?

I joke with my students that older poets focus on only a few images: trees, birds, and flowers. After becoming pope didn't pan out, ornithologist seemed like my next, logical career path. I had (have) all the field guides and records of various bird songs. From an early age, I felt at home on a trail, waiting for birds to flit past so I could identify them.

I'm of the mind that birds are unavoidable in poems. Look out the window. Search for a word. Wait a moment. There goes a bird. Whatever line you're writing, a bird jumps into it. The stories of the saints feel more folklorish in my poems than birds. Birds are a way of life. I'm astounded by them, their flight patterns, their songs, their migrations. This past summer in Iceland, I watched as a puffin dropped under the clear water and jetted below the surface, smashing the surface with a beak of tiny, silver fish. While their stubby wings aren't so great in the air, they serve as quite the propellant within the sea.

Bees in their abundance are a fairly recent addition to my poems. Five or so years ago, we had a series of gardens installed in our backyard. Perhaps it's a sign of age, but I'm gardening with joy—smiling when the monarch butterflies visit the blooms. Even the flowers of weeds have earned their rightful place within the array of "official" flowers. Besides, the bees don't care about the origin of the flower, or how humans categorize them—just that the flower has something to offer them. The poem "daycare in the garden of good children" addresses the "gardening" phase of my married life. We share the relief of a spring shower.

Another thing that drew me to this collection is that it's such a tender portrait of long marriage. What makes a good love poem?

What makes a good love poem? Leave it unread. But if I decide otherwise, I make certain each word serves the desire to reveal the intimacy of love. The poem then becomes a touchstone for the version of love I felt in that moment. Robert Browning succinctly ends "Love Among the Ruins" with "Love is best." Shakespeare didn't do any better than that. No one has. I am where I am today because my wife chose me when I chose her. I was a college reject when we met and she waited for me to figure things out. I'm not sure how she found the patience. It takes a good deal of maintenance to keep love's pulse steady.

Val is strong-willed and smart. I rely on her when it comes to financial decisions or even on matters of what an adult might wear to dinner. And yet, for reasons that make no sense to me, she trusts my ability to know when it's going to rain or merely threaten to rain. A few times each summer, while walking the dog, the three of us are caught in a downpour. We walk it out, no need to hurry. There's trust that even in my weather forecasting failure, we'll make it home. The collection ends with "waiting to speak." Every word of that poem is the three of us in the rain. I see us calm in the rain. Rain calm and together.

What about love and life do we inherit from our parents? To me, this feels like another way to interpret the title *say, said*: what was and what is now, or, as you say, "*say 'said' and i'll remember a single word calls the past back to the living.*" How do we filter and understand the past or our own beginnings? You capture this so beautifully. Did this inform the way you structured the book? What led you to choose this as a title?

The book tiptoes around my mother…until it doesn't. She's in "tonight's the night," the first poem in the collection. She dresses me in drag for Halloween. My mother anchors the first third of the poems and then pops in and out of the remaining poems. Her last appearance is in "a valley away/ hailey, idaho." In that poem, the blood of a dead deer reassures the narrator, telling him, "your mother's here with us."

My mother passed away in spring 2023. Our dog, Earl, left us a few months after that. And Judy, my mother-in-law, a few days after Earl. It was all too much. You find yourself living with the dead in a past that's as timeless as the future. My mother was a difficult person, but we did our best. I gave her that line, the title of the manuscript, as a belated show of respect—for all she did for me as a mother—gifting me my past and future. To move forward, I reconciled the often overlooked good within all that difficulty. My mother was first to notice my interest in poetry. She took note I was coming home from the grade school library with Whitman and Dr. Seuss, and bought me my first book of poetry. I still have it.

Your book contains no section breaks, even though it covers a large span of time, childhood to now. Everything seems to exist at once. Could you explain this choice for readers?

This manuscript represents ten years of writing and sixty years of life. It has featured maybe ten different titles, reams of poems that have come and gone. There have been sections that were set apart by shapes—a triangle, a box, a circle, and a rhombus. I placed the poems into the corresponding shapes. The poem "triangle tavern," fit nicely, but then I just started making excuses to have certain poems fit certain shapes. A few years ago, an editor said that the chapters were too much of a distraction. So, I tried something different.

My guess is that all first books are the summation of a poet's life to that point. When my mother passed, I envisioned a narrative structure that wasn't so "year-by-year" obvious. There's growth in these poems, but not necessarily growth in a forward trajectory. The failed future pope spends a bit of time in bars, follows the flight of monarch butterflies, and shouts when a black and white warbler lights on a tree in the backyard. I've come to accept this book is not about me. Maybe these ten years were spent figuring that important aspect out. Our lives are measured by our interactions with other people and places and birds and dogs and flowers and bees. This is a collection of poems about interactions and the voices that rise up and seal the interactions in its amber.

This collection feels personal but avoids feeling too much like memoir or navel gazing. Was this a concern for you as you wrote these poems? Do you have advice for poets who want to tell the story of their lives while appealing to a larger audience?

In an interview from a while back, Adrian Matejka said something along the lines of his poetry improved when he realized he didn't have to be the hero in his poems. I took that to heart and immediately reduced the "I" to "i" in the poems and then made certain the various voices in the poems put the narrative voice in its place (occasionally). I'm self-deprecating in my life outside of poetry, so it feels like a good way to empower the narrator of these poems. Life isn't always that serious. And don't worry about appealing to any audience. Be yourself. Be true. Someone will listen. And if you're lucky, a few others will listen as well.

A final theme I noticed here, as a female writer, is masculinity—what it's

built on and how it's changed over time and for the speaker. With its Western imagery, it almost feels like the "Wild West." What do you hope your readers take away about American masculinity?

I'm thankful for this observation and question. I was fortunate to be raised by good, male role models: my father, my Paw-Paw, my uncles Bill, Mike, and Gary—and later, my father-in-law Bill. But it's women who have filled in the lessons that men don't always teach to other men. If I'm a decent man, it's because of the women in my life. Most important, when the women in my life have educated me, I listened. My mother taught me self-reliance at a young age. In no uncertain terms, she eradicated the expectations that a wife would "take care of me." She set my brother and I up to be equal partners in our relationships. It's a heck of a gift she gave us—even though it's such an obvious, logical, and simple thing for a man to know.

What draws me most to the poetry of Terrance Hayes is his take on masculinity. "At Pegasus," the introductory poem in Hayes' first collection, *Muscular Music*, tells the story of a straight man at a gay club, admitting, "I'm just here for the music." But then the narrator reveals, "But I have held/ a boy on my back before." What matters most to the narrator is the music, wherever he finds it. But he also realizes that the bodies moving to the music are just as important. It matters to the narrator to say clearly that male on male skin is natural and celebratory. The narrator's memory of carrying his injured friend is a moment of human ecstasy not much different than the men at the club dancing to the universality of music. When I asked myself why I loved Hayes' poetry so much, I arrived upon some obvious things: the imaginative depth of the poems, the twisting and turning narratives, the inventiveness of form, and the wide-ranging and essential subject matter, all those sounds upon sounds. But "At Pegasus" held the reason—Hayes' poems offer a new kind of masculinity, one that's always been here. Hayes' poems legitimize a masculinity that's open and inclusive and non-threatening. I'm hoping some of that type of masculinity is sensed in my poetry as well.

Your poems certainly achieve this. They feel wide-ranging, essential, funny, and inventive all in, as you say, a "non-threatening" way. As a fellow poet, your journey with this book, the depth of your thought, is inspiring. Maggie Smith said that each revision should get "closer to the poem we sense is there, waiting." Your voice, with all its humor and wisdom, is so clear in this version, I can't imagine anything else to be true. I get the sense that all this also is deeply connected to your teaching. How does teaching inform the way you write/revise, and vice versa?

The cover letter for my poetry submissions begins, "I'm a husband to my wife Valerie, and a father to our good dog, Trixie." Husband is the primary way that I self-identify. Second to husband is teacher. I didn't plan on becoming a teacher. After earning my M.A. from the University of North Florida, I was asked to adjunct a class in fall 1997. I fought against it, shaking my head that they would even ask. But Dr. Kathy Hassall kept after me, called a few times and I finally agreed. She thought I'd be a good teacher and I trusted her. Sometimes the right people are there at the right times in our lives, and if we listen to them, our lives change irrevocably for the better. As I had been warned, teaching hammered away at my creative drive. But when I agreed to teach an Introduction to Poetry Writing class, I was more or less shamed back into writing my own poems. How could I teach a craft I wasn't practicing? It can be argued that I write only because I teach. I do my best to create a classroom atmosphere where I'm not perceived as the master of my craft. It's important that the poets view me as a fellow writer, someone struggling with language like they do. I don't have children of my own, so I'm grateful for my nearly rejected vocation. Teaching is a privilege. Semester by semester, I lecture and grade, and grade some more, but I also interact and learn from the brightest minds, witness as their writing gains clarity and depth. It's thrilling when a young poet shares with me the news that a poem of theirs has been accepted for publication. That kind of student success is far more exhilarating than any accolades my writing has received.

Finally, you mentioned earlier that most first books are a "greatest hits," of sorts, they are, often, a culmination of many years of work. I wholeheartedly agree. What about second books? What's next for you?

I have three manuscripts in various degrees of completion. There's a collection of poems based around music. I have been working on this manuscript the longest. My goal is to write 100 rough draft poems before I begin the arduous process of editing each of them into shape.

The second manuscript is still in the planning stages. When my mother passed away a couple years ago, I pocketed her handwritten recipes—about 40 different concoctions. The interesting thing is that my mom did not cook. My parents were in a "gourmet club" in the 70s and my mom would locate and copy down recipes for dishes she'd cooked for gourmet club—but not the family. The plan for this collection is to have each recipe become a poem—from the grocery shopping to the cooking and consumption, the conversations with my wife as she watches me flail and fail. It's a strange way to connect with my mother, but I'm looking forward to that endeavor when I get the necessary time.

The third manuscript is based on an in-process, yearlong secular experience of going back to Catholic mass after 45 years. In December of 2024, I accompanied my Aunt Carol to mass in New Orleans. It was odd to be back within the rituals, to find what I remembered and what I had forgotten. The church was St. Mary's in the Irish Channel. My Maw-Maw was baptized there, received her first communion there. The old priest bored me to death with his homily, but I felt an unexpected peace in the old pew. When I got back to Jax, I looked up a local Catholic church and have been attending mass every Sunday since. Again, my experience is mostly secular. I'm not taking the sacraments (don't tell the priest). I'm just sitting in a pew, listening closely to everything. Peaceful. Each mass is a poem. I'm giving this return to church a year to play itself out, to see what I find, to see where I'll go from there. When finished, I'll have 50-60 poems that reflect on and deviate from a single mass. Perhaps it's a sin to use the mass as a way into a series of poems, but as *say, says* reveals, the Catholic part of me is far from resolved.

NOTES

"what the florentine hid from us": In 2021, museum conservators in England uncovered what they believed *might* be Michelangelo's fingerprint. Said fingerprint was found within a small-scale model used for a larger sculpture—the tomb of Pope Julius II. Intact, small-scale models of Michelangelo's work are rare. They were usually broken after use. Samael is an archangel often associated with death and destruction. He is also thought to be connected to the serpent in the Garden of Eden.

"agnes in the flood": My Maw-Maw passed away right before Hurricane Katrina hit New Orleans. She was the last family member to go into the O'Regan family plot and the above ground burial site was uncapped at the time of the flood. The family was worried that Maw-Maw's casket would float free as so many other caskets had done during the flood. Thankfully, her casket stayed in place, but I decided to let her out for an adventure. My Maw-Maw never drove a car, so I romanticized her floating through her old neighborhoods, waving to neighbors, signing the cross as she floated past churches. Saint Adjutor is the patron saint of boaters and swimmers. Jean Laffitte was a pirate that did some good during the Battle of New Orleans. He is also the hero to many a child who grew up mesmerized by the stories of his exploits. Saint Blaise is the patron saint of matters of the throat. For Catholics, there is a feast of Saint Blaise where you can get your throat blessed—to ward off choking on fish bones. I went to church three times on that day. Saint Chrisotpher is the patron saint of travelers.

"st. edna and the thieves": For years, I've been entranced by a famous photograph of Edna St. Vincent Millay—the one where she stands within a circle of Japanese magnolia branches. John Muir once said something along the lines that Hetch Hetchy was even more beautiful than Yosemite Valley. The government flooded Hetch Hetchy for a water reservoir.

"teach violinists to stage dive": There are some parts of Mendelssohn that are outright punk. I don't understand how violinists sit still, contain all that aggression. There's a YouTube video of Gwendolyn Brooks discussing "We Real Cool." She tells us the poem was banned for her usage of the word "jazz." She says that in some of the prevailing brains of that time, "jazz" held sexual connotations. No group cheers for themselves quite like a room of space engineers.

"falling is the last resort of squirrels": During our COVID home boundedness, I buried a dead squirrel in the alley behind our house. My neighbor, Kenston, built a cross for him, hung a necklace around the cross. Some of our neighbors thought our dog, Earl, had died, so they placed votive candles around the grave of a squirrel that took an unfortunate spill from our oak tree. With the world in such flux, that little grave, and the squirrel buried there, meant something to all of us who walked by it.

"gifts of unexpected conveyances": I'm not sure how one drops a book of poetry into a bag of turmeric, but someone did, and given the seedier side of Levis' story, a poem was born. A ghost of a dj, somewhere in Tallahassee, introduced me to the music of Merle Haggard. I wish I could love one thing as much as he loved each MH song he spun. I tried to duplicate that late night radio station experience, driving through Tallahassee at the witching hour, but it never happened again. If my wife wasn't there with me, I'd doubt it even happened.

"everything from one": St. Lous Cemetery No. 1 might be the most famous of New Orleans' storied cemeteries. It's been used in countless movies—*Easy Rider* in particular. Among many inhabitants, it's the final resting place of Homer Plessy, musicians Ernie K-Doe and Earl King, and the jazz pioneer and cornetist Isadore Barbarin. The evil and sadistic Delphine LaLaurie is there, but perhaps the most famous resident is the Voodoo Queen, Marie Laveau. It is thought that if you place three Xs on her grave, she'll grant you a wish. If you Google the cemetery, though, an image of the "new" and future tomb of Nicholas Cage is what pops up. And it's true, I was there with a class, and when the docent was busy docenting, the pyramid tomb still under construction, I crawled within its chamber.

"bartram heard it": William Bartram's *Travels* should be required reading for those in Florida—in particular, for those who live in close proximity to the St. Johns River. His stories of sleeping on the river bank, awakened by numerous alligators advancing upon him are spinetingling—though I'm not sure sleeping within reach of alligators qualifies as adventurous or heroic. And yes, there were those intelligent few who once proffered birds migrated to the moon. I hope they do.

"a place to sit a spell": Moe, Larry, and Curly, the Three Stooges, had this bit where one of them would offer his closed fist to another stooge and say, "you see that?" Sometimes that fist was used as a distraction to bonk the unsuspecting stooge with the other fist. But oftentimes, when given the question, "you see that?" the confronted stooge would just slap the hand and around the hand would go, and what head it would land on was anyone's guess. This a poem for unanswered questions, where action becomes an answer.

"marsh hawk": A plumber doing some work on our first house noticed my copy of Tim O'Brien's *The Things They Carried*. He asked if I was reading it. I told him I was teaching it to a class of college freshmen. He motioned me out to his truck, said he has something to show me. He was a Vietnam Vet and had only recently found his way out of a never-ending bottle of whisky. He drew the scene on the truck's toolbox, in the dirt, said, "Here's a story for those freshmen," and he described walking into a peaceful valley, grass swaying in the light breeze. The most beautiful thing he'd ever seen, he said. Until they marched closer and the swaying grass transformed into a sea of maggots moving across the bodies of dead Viet Cong troops.

"if you need a revolution, dee dee ramone can count you down": Live, The Ramones' bass player, Dee Dee Ramone, would aggressively count the band into each song. If I could have only one alarm clock, it'd be Dee Dee Ramone standing on the side of my bed, counting me awake through a Marshall stack.

"a coin awaits a sailor": Legend has it that the bar at The Old Point House in East Angle Bay, Wales, has a few coins shellacked to its surface, left there eons ago by a sailor, a pirate heading to sea—a little bounty for his children should he not return. The "legend" was told to us by a fellow hiker on the Pembrokeshire Coastal Trail. We walked by that old bar—like 16th century old, but to my regret, didn't check out the legend. We had some tough miles in our legs that evening and flagons of cold milk awaiting us.

"mid-november flower": Joan Miro was a Spanish artist. You know when you know the art you like. His surrealistic paintings charge my brain like few other artists.

"waiting to speak": A poem about rain and my wife and our dog, Earl. It's no coincidence that his name is the only capitalized word within the collection of poems.

ACKNOWLEDGEMENTS

"a hive for water" *Barnstorm Journal*, 2019
"three minutes" *Bridge Eight*, 2019
"the luminaria sleep" *Chiron Review*, 2015
"a barstool at st. nick's" *Clackamas Literary Review*, 2017
"marsh hawk" *Cobalt Review*, 2020
"tin ceiling sky" *convivium journal*, 2020
"abattoir," and "daycare in the garden of good children" *Delta Poetry Review*, 2021
"children" *Dunes Review*, 2016
"agnes in the flood" and "marriage house" *Forge*, 2014
"sweatshirt of bees" *Free State Review*, 2019
"everything from one," "roadkill bingo," "the coin awaits a sailor," and "waiting to speak" *Ginosko Literary Journal*, 2018
"she who carries the water, carries the fish" *Glassworks Magazine*, 2019
"rock by rock" and "magnolias" *Mistake House Magazine*, 2018
"downs lounge" *Permafrost*, 2017
"meteors over hurricane ridge" *Raleigh Review*, 2016
"fishing poem," "bartram heard it," and "vagary" *River Heron Review* (2020, 2020, 2021)
"acorn tattoo" *Rogue Agent*, 2017
"these trails never wanted us" *Rumble Fish Quarterly*, 2018
"trails in our legs" *Salt Hill Journal*, 2025
"if you need a revolution, dee dee ramone'll count you down" *Saranac Review*, 2020
"gifts of unexpected conveyances" *Spillway*, 2021
"saliva's point of jumping off" *Split Rock Review*, 2019
"what we picked on our way" *Stirring: A Literary Collection*, 2015
"geometric matter(s)" *The Evansville Review*, 2018.
"tonight's the night" and "we are told bay leaves" *The Jacksonvillain*, 2023
"a heralding" *The Summerset Review*, 2017
"the boy who would be pope" *Tipton Poetry Journal*, 2019

"marriage house," "the luminaria sleeps," "what we picked on our way," and "agnes in the flood" appear in the audio chapbook *The Dream of Blue Moon Flowers* published by *EAT Poems* (2016)

"magnolias," "the boy who would be pope," "downs lounge," "geometric matter(s)," "a barstool at st. nick's," "a hive for water," "gifts of unexpected conveyances," "motorboat mels," and "daycare at the garden of good children" appear in the audio chapbook *A Boy's Pirating Eye* published by *EAT Poems* (2022)

"waiting to speak" is quoted in the musical composition "waiting to speak" by Nicole Knorr (*North Star Music, LLC.* 2024)

THANKS

and so much appreciation to James McNulty and Sara Moore Wagner at *Driftwood Press* for finding something worth remembering in these hard-earned poems.

to my Mom, who gave me my first book of poems and believed in me.

to my Dad, the enigmatic hero in many of these poems. You taught me each step's an adventure not to be missed.

to David, me and you on Sunday mornings—a record store instead of a church.

and love to my whole family, but in particular Aunt Carol & Uncle Bill who have encouraged my poetry and helped guide my life in every way.

to Val, who knows when old Hagg sings a song, it stays sung. Here's to our long song.

to Seamus Owen, David MacKinnon, & Russ Turney, our friendship is the ballast.

to Brian, Jerry, & Ted, I'm with you in my dreams.

to Amanda Forester, Michael Phelps, & Matt Mobley, you helped make the MFA days some of the best in my life.

to Bill Slaughter & Kathy Hassall, for your teaching and mentorship. You convinced me I could make a life as a teacher.

to Sandra Beasley, Alan Michael Parker, & Erica Dawson, MFA mentors and poets extraordinaire.

to Mark Ari & Linda Howell, who refused to let my teacher life extinguish the poet part.

to Barrett Warner, a careful reader and editor who nudged this book along through the years.

to all my students, it's true
it shouldn't be
i learned more from you
than you did from me

to my boy, Earl. I hate the way we left things. I hope I get a chance to make it up to you.

Photography by Russ Turney

Fred Dale is a husband to his wife, Valerie, a father to his good dog, Miss Trixie, and a faculty member in the Department of English at the University of North Florida. He holds an MFA from the University of Tampa, but mostly, he just grade papers. His work has appeared in *Spillway, Sugar House Review, Salt Hill Journal, The Summerset Review, Tipton Poetry Journal*, and others. He has published two audio chapbooks: *The Dream of Blue Moon Flowers* and *A Boy's Pirating Eye*. Three of his poems have been nominated for a Pushcart Prize.

MORE TITLES FROM
DRIFTWOOD PRESS

comics, fiction, poetry
chapbooks & collections

www.ingramcontent.com/pod-product-compliance
Lightning Source LLC
Chambersburg PA
CBHW081432070526
44586CB00020B/2556